Open Your Heart

Open Your Heart

DAILY LENTEN REFLECTIONS
WITH

Pope Francis

Edited by Theresa Khoo

BOOKS & MEDIA

Boston

Library of Congress Cataloging-in-Publication Data

Names: Francis, Pope, 1936- author. | Khoo, Theresa, editor.

Title: Open your heart : daily Lenten reflections with Pope Francis / edited by Theresa Khoo.

Description: Boston : Pauline Books & Media, [2019] | "Excerpts from Pope Francis's audiences, homilies, Angelus messages, addresses, messages and exhortations"-- T.p. verso.

Identifiers: LCCN 2018030644| ISBN 9780819855084 (pbk.) | ISBN 0819855081 (pbk.)

Subjects: LCSH: Lent--Prayers and devotions. | Catholic Church--Prayers and devotions. | Catholic Church--Doctrines.

Classification: LCC BX2170.L4 F728 2019 | DDC 242/.34--dc23

LC record available at https://lccn.loc.gov/2018030644

Excerpts from Pope Francis's audiences, homilies, angelus messages, addresses, messages, and exhortations copyright © Libreria Editrice Vaticana. Used with permission.

The Scripture quotations contained in the excerpts from Pope Francis are taken directly from Pope Francis's works.

All other Scripture quotations contained herein are from the *New Revised Standard Version Bible: Catholic Edition,* copyright © 1989, 1993, Division of Christian Education of the National Council of the Churches of Christ in the United States of America. Used by permission. All rights reserved.

Cover design by Rosana Usselmann

Cover photo by [contact design department or business office for information]

Published by Pauline Books & Media, 50 Saint Paul's Avenue, Boston, MA 02130–3491

Printed in the U.S.A.

www.pauline.org

Pauline Books & Media is the publishing house of the Daughters of St. Paul, an international congregation of women religious serving the Church with the communications media.

1 2 3 4 5 6 7 8 9   23 22 21 20 19

Contents

A Change of Heart

Be Reconciled to God

We urge you also not to accept the grace of God in vain.

—2 Corinthians 6:2

The Lord never tires of having mercy on us, and wants to offer us his forgiveness once again, inviting us to return to him with a new heart, purified of evil, purified by tears, to take part in his joy. How should we accept this invitation? Saint Paul advises us: "We entreat you on behalf of Christ, be reconciled to God" (2 Cor 5:20). This power of conversion is not only the work of mankind; it is letting oneself be reconciled. Reconciliation between us and God is possible thanks to the mercy of the Father who, out of love for us, did not hesitate to sacrifice his only begotten Son. Indeed Christ, who was just and without sin, was made to be sin (see v. 21) when, on the cross, he took on the burden of our sins, and in this way he redeemed and justified us before God. "In him" we can become just, in him we can change, if we accept the grace of God and do not allow this "acceptable time" to pass in vain (6:2). Please, let us stop, let us stop a while and let ourselves be reconciled to God.

Homily, February 18, 2015

REFLECTION

How can I be reconciled to God this Lent?

PRAYER

Lord, help me stop and consciously open my heart to your grace and mercy.

Opening the Door of Our Hearts

Choose life so that you and your descendants may live, loving the LORD your God, obeying him, and holding fast to him.

—Deuteronomy 30:19–20

The first step on the Christian path . . . entails entering through the open door which is Christ, where he, the Savior, awaits us and offers us a new and joyful life.

There may be a few obstacles, which close the door of the heart. There is the temptation to lock the doors, or to live with our sin, minimizing it, always justifying it, thinking we are no worse than others. This, however, is how the locks of the soul are closed and we remain shut inside, prisoners of evil. Another obstacle is the *shame of opening* the secret door of the heart. Shame, in reality, is a good symptom, because it shows that we want to break away from evil; however, it must never be transformed into apprehension or fear. There is a third pitfall, that of *distancing ourselves from the door* . . . when we hide in our misery, when we ruminate constantly. . . . This happens because we stay alone with ourselves, closing ourselves off and avoiding the light; while the Lord's grace alone frees us. Therefore let us be reconciled, let us listen to Jesus who says to those who are weary and oppressed: "Come to me" (Mt 11:28). Not to dwell within themselves, but to go to him! Comfort and peace are there.

Homily, February 10, 2016

REFLECTION

What obstacles prevent me from opening the door of my heart to Christ?

PRAYER

Help me see myself honestly, Lord, and remove whatever blocks me from you.

Three Remedies for Sin

Seek good and not evil, that you may live; and so the
LORD, the God of hosts, will be with you.

—Amos 5:14

The Gospel . . . calls us to be protagonists, embracing
three remedies, three medicines which heal us
from sin (see Mt 6:1–6, 16–18).

In the first place is *prayer*, an expression of openness
and trust in the Lord; it is the personal encounter with
him, which shortens the distances created by sin. Praying
means saying: "I am not self-sufficient, I need you; *you*
are my life and my salvation." In the second place is *charity*, in order to overcome our lack of involvement with
regard to others. True love, in fact, is not an outward act;
it is not giving something in a paternalistic way in order

to assuage the conscience, but to accept those who are in need of our time, our friendship, our help. It means living to serve, overcoming the temptation to satisfy ourselves. In the third place is *fasting*, penance, in order to free ourselves from dependencies regarding what is passing, and to train ourselves to be more sensitive and merciful. It is an invitation to simplicity and to sharing: to take something from our table and from our assets in order to once again find the true benefit of freedom.

Homily, February 10, 2016

REFLECTION

How do I extend myself in love and service of others?

PRAYER

Lord, may I respond to your call to love through sincere acts of self-giving toward my brothers and sisters.

Saturday after Ash Wednesday

Finding Our Christian Identity

We know that our old self was crucified with him so that the body of sin might be destroyed, and we might no longer be enslaved to sin.

—Romans 6:6

Jesus calls us to live prayer, charity, and penance with consistency and authenticity, overcoming hypocrisy. May Lent be a beneficial time to "prune" falseness, worldliness, indifference: so as not to think that everything is fine if I am fine; so as to understand that what counts is not approval, the search for success or consensus, but the cleansing of the heart and of life; so as to find again our Christian identity, namely, *the love that serves, not the selfishness that serves us.* Let us embark on the journey together, as Church . . . and keeping our gaze fixed on the crucifix. He, loving us, invites us to be reconciled with God and to return to him, in order to find ourselves again.

Homily, February 10, 2016

REFLECTION

How can I live more authentically as a disciple of Jesus?

PRAYER

Cleanse me of self-righteousness and hypocrisy, Lord, and help me seek my deepest identity in you.

WEEK 1

Entering the Path of Lent

Fight Satan with the Word of God

And the Spirit immediately drove him out into the wilderness. He was in the wilderness forty days, tempted by Satan; and he was with the wild beasts; and the angels waited on him.

—Mark 1:12–13

Lent is *a time of combat! A spiritual combat against the spirit of evil.* And while we cross the Lenten "desert," we keep our gaze[s] fixed upon Easter, which is the definitive victory of Jesus against the Evil One, against sin and against death. This is the meaning of this First Sunday of Lent: to place ourselves decisively on the path of Jesus, the road that leads to life. . . .

This path of Jesus passes through *the desert.* The desert is the place where *the voice of God and the voice of the tempter can be heard.* . . . And how do we hear the voice of God? We hear it in his word. For this reason, it is important to know Scripture, because otherwise we do not know how to react to the snares of the Evil One. And here I would like to return to my advice of reading the Gospel every day.... Meditate on it for a little while, for ten minutes. And also carry it with you in your pocket or your purse. . . . But always have the Gospel at hand. The Lenten desert helps us to say "no" to worldliness, to "idols"; it helps us to make courageous choices in accordance with the Gospel and to strengthen solidarity with the brothers.

Angelus, February 22, 2015

REFLECTION

Can I make an effort to read and reflect on the Scriptures each day?

PRAYER

In the struggle of daily life, let me find courage and light in your holy word.

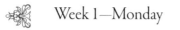

The Breath of Life

See, now is the acceptable time; see, now is the day of salvation!

—2 Corinthians 6:2

Lent is a path; it leads to the triumph of mercy over all that would crush us or reduce us to something unworthy of our dignity as God's children. Lent is the road leading from slavery to freedom, from suffering to joy, from death to life.... We are dust in the loving hands of God, who has breathed his spirit of life upon each one of us, and still wants to do so. He wants to keep giving us that *breath of life* that saves us from every other type of breath: the stifling *asphyxia* brought on by our selfishness, the stifling asphyxia generated by petty ambition and silent indifference—an asphyxia that smothers the spirit, narrows our horizons, and slows the beating of our hearts. The breath of God's life saves us from this asphyxia that dampens our faith, cools our charity, and strangles every hope. To experience Lent is to yearn for this breath of life that our Father unceasingly offers us amid the mire of our history. . . . Lent is the time to start breathing again.

Homily, March 1, 2017

REFLECTION

How is the Lord inviting me to freedom from any selfish ambitions I may have?

PRAYER

Help me breathe deeply of your life-giving spirit, Lord, and respond to you with generosity and joy.

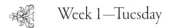
Saying No to Indifference and Exclusion

The LORD is near to the brokenhearted, and saves the crushed in spirit.

—Psalm 34:18

Lent is the time for saying no. No to the spiritual asphyxia born of the pollution caused by indifference, by thinking that other people's lives are not my concern, and by every attempt to trivialize life, especially the lives of those whose flesh is burdened by so much superficiality. Lent means saying no to the toxic pollution of empty and meaningless words, of harsh and hasty criticism, of simplistic analyses that fail to grasp the complexity of problems, especially the problems of those who suffer the most. Lent is the time to say no to the asphyxia of a prayer that soothes our conscience, of an almsgiving that leaves us self-satisfied, of a fasting that makes us feel good. Lent is the time to say no to the asphyxia born of relationships that exclude, that try to find God while avoiding the wounds of Christ present in the wounds of his brothers and sisters: in a word, all those forms of spirituality that reduce the faith to a ghetto culture, a culture of exclusion.

Homily, March 1, 2017

REFLECTION

Do I keep others at a safe distance, especially those who may be wounded or in pain?

PRAYER

I hear your challenge, Lord, to see you in every fragile or broken person I encounter. May I welcome and reverence every suffering brother and sister.

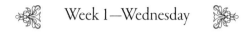

We Are God's Beloved Children

[Baptism] now saves you—not as a removal of dirt from the body, but as an appeal to God for a good conscience.

—1 Peter 3:21

Lent . . . is a special time for recalling the gift of our baptism, when we became children of God. The Church invites us to renew the gift she has given us, not to let this gift lie dormant as if it were something from the past or locked away in a "memory chest." Lent is a good time to recover the joy and hope that make us feel like beloved sons and daughters of the Father. The Father waits for us in order to cast off our garments of exhaustion, of apathy, of mistrust, and so clothe us with the dignity that only a true father or mother knows how to give their children, with the garments born of tenderness and love.

Our Father—he is the Father of a great family; he is our Father. He knows that he has a unique love, but he does not know how to bear or raise an "only child." He is the God of the home, of brotherhood, of bread broken and shared. He is the God who is "Our Father," not "my father" or "your stepfather."

God's dream makes its home and lives in each one of us so that at every Easter, in every Eucharist we celebrate, we may be the children of God.

Homily, February 14, 2016

REFLECTION

How do I behave as a family member to each person in God's family?

PRAYER

Lord, your family encompasses all peoples. May I treat everyone I meet as brother and sister.

Our Three Temptations

Cast away from you all the transgressions that you have committed against me, and get yourselves a new heart and a new spirit!

—Ezekiel 18:31

Lent is a time . . . for letting our eyes be opened to the frequent injustices that stand in direct opposition to the dream and the plan of God. It is a time to unmask three great temptations that wear down and fracture the image God wanted to form in us. . . .

First, wealth: seizing hold of goods destined for all, and using them only for "my own people." That is, taking "bread" based on the toil of others, or even at the expense of their very lives. That wealth which tastes of pain, bitterness, and suffering. That is the bread that a corrupt family or society gives its own children.

The second temptation, vanity: the pursuit of prestige based on continuous, relentless exclusion of those who "are not like me." The futile chasing of those five minutes of fame, which do not forgive the "reputation" of others.

"Making firewood from a felled tree" gradually gives way to the third temptation, the worst. It is that of pride, or rather, putting oneself on a higher level than one truly is on, feeling that one does not share the life of "mere mortals," and yet being one who prays every day: "I thank you, Lord, that you have not made me like those others. . . ."

[These are] three temptations that the Christian is faced with daily, three temptations that seek to corrode, destroy, and extinguish the joy and freshness of the Gospel.

Homily, February 14, 2016

REFLECTION

Which of these three temptations afflict me?

PRAYER

Lord, give me the strength to confront the truth about myself, and the humility to ask for help from you.

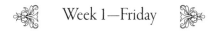
Our God of Mercy

For with the LORD there is steadfast love, and with him is great power to redeem.

—Psalm 130:7

We have opted for Jesus and not for the devil; we want to follow in Jesus' footsteps, even though we know that this is not easy. We know what it means to be seduced by money, fame, and power. For this reason, the Church gives us the gift of this Lenten season, invites us to conversion, offering but one certainty: *he* is waiting for us and wants to heal our hearts of all that tears us down. He is the God who has a name: Mercy. His name is our wealth; his name is what makes us famous; his name is our power, and in his name we say once more with the psalm: "You are my God and in you I trust."

May the Holy Spirit renew in us the certainty that his name is Mercy, and may he let us experience each day that "the Gospel fills the hearts and lives of all who encounter Jesus," knowing that "with Christ and in Christ joy is constantly born anew" (see *Evangelii Gaudium*, n. 1).

Homily, February 14, 2016

REFLECTION

How much do I trust in God's merciful love for me?

PRAYER

Loving God, help me to reject the temptations of the world and return to you.

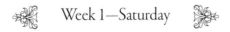
The Good News of the Gospel

The Spirit of the Lord is upon me, because he has anointed me to bring good news to the poor.

—Luke 4:18

Jesus, anointed by the Spirit, brings good news to the poor. Everything he proclaims . . . is *good news*. News full of the joy of the Gospel—the joy of those anointed in their sins with the oil of forgiveness and anointed in their charism with the oil of mission, in order to anoint others in turn. . . .

The phrase "*good news*" might appear as just another way of saying "the Gospel." Yet those words point to something essential: the joy of the Gospel. The Gospel is good news because it is, in essence, a message of joy.

The *good news* is the precious pearl of which we read in the Gospel. It is not a thing but a mission. This is evident to anyone who has experienced the "delightful and comforting joy of evangelizing" (*Evangelii Gaudium*, 10)....

Good news. A single word—Gospel—that, even as it is spoken, becomes truth, brimming with joy and mercy. We should never attempt to separate these three graces of the Gospel: its truth, which is non-negotiable; its mercy, which is unconditional and offered to all sinners; and its joy, which is personal and open to everyone. Truth, mercy, and joy: these three go together.

Homily, April 13, 2017

REFLECTION

Is the gospel "good news" in my life? Do I share this good news or keep it to myself?

PRAYER

Lord, may I bring the truth, mercy, and joy of the good news to everyone I meet.

WEEK 2

Jesus Saves Us from Our Sins

To Love Like Christ

"This is my Son, the Beloved; listen to him!"

—Mark 9:7

Jesus reveals himself as the perfect icon of the Father, the radiance of his glory. He is the fulfillment of revelation; that is why beside him . . . Moses and Elijah appear. They represent the Law and the Prophets, so as to signify that everything finishes and begins in Jesus, in his passion and in his glory.

Their instructions for the disciples and for us is this: "Listen to him!" . . . To listen to Christ, in fact, entails *taking up the logic of his Paschal Mystery*, setting out on the journey with him to make of oneself a gift of love to others . . . with an attitude of detachment from worldly things and of interior freedom. One must, in other words, be willing to "lose one's very life" (see Mk 8:35), by giving it up so that all men might be saved. . . . There will always be a cross . . . but at the end we are always led to happiness. Jesus does not deceive us. He promised us happiness and will give it to us if we follow his ways.

With Peter, James, and John we too climb the Mount of the Transfiguration today and stop in contemplation of the face of Jesus, to retrieve the message and translate it into our lives, for we too can be transfigured by love.

Angelus, March 1, 2015

REFLECTION

How can I be a gift of love to others?

PRAYER

Lord, help me listen to you and give of myself to those in need.

The Cross as a Symbol of Christian Faith

Then Jesus told his disciples, "If any want to become my followers, let them deny themselves and take up their cross and follow me."

—Matthew 16:24

Those who die with Jesus shall rise again with Jesus. The cross is the door to resurrection. Whoever struggles alongside him will triumph with him. This is the message of hope contained in Jesus' cross, urging us to be strong.... The Christian cross ... is a call to the love with which Jesus sacrificed himself to save humanity from evil and sin.

In this Lenten season, we contemplate with devotion the image of the crucifix, Jesus on the cross; this is the symbol of Christian faith, the emblem of Jesus, who died and rose for us. Let us ensure that the cross marks the stages of our Lenten journey in order to understand ever better the seriousness of sin and the value of the sacrifice by which the Savior has saved us all.

The Blessed Virgin was able to contemplate the glory of Jesus hidden in his humanness. May she help us stay with him in silent prayer, to allow ourselves to be enlightened by his presence, so as to bring a reflection of his glory to our hearts through the darkest nights.

Angelus, March 12, 2017

REFLECTION

What are the crosses I am carrying? Will I allow Jesus to help me with them?

PRAYER

Lord, help me to embrace my crosses as a mark of my sorrow and sacrifice and also as a sign of solidarity with you who loved us to your death.

Cleansing the Temple of Self-Interest

"Stop making my Father's house a marketplace!"

—John 2:16

A disciple of Jesus does not go to Church simply to observe a precept, to feel he or she is in good standing with God ... "But Lord, I go every Sunday ... don't interfere in my life, don't disturb me." ... A disciple of Jesus goes to Church to encounter the Lord and to find, in his grace operating in the sacraments, the power to think and act according to the Gospel. This is why we cannot mislead ourselves of being able to enter the Lord's house and "cover up," with prayer and acts of devotion, conduct contrary to the requirements of justice, honesty, and charity to our neighbor. ...

It is instead about fulfilling an itinerary of conversion and atonement, to remove the remnants of sin, as Jesus did, cleansing the temple of wretched interests. *Lent is the appropriate time for all of this* . . . the time at which we are called to rediscover the Sacrament of Penance and Reconciliation, which lets us pass from the shadows of sin to the light of grace and of friendship with Jesus. The great power this sacrament has in Christian life . . . enables us to grow in union with God, and lets us reacquire lost joy and experience the comfort of feeling personally held in God's merciful embrace.

Homily, March 7, 2015

REFLECTION

What is my motivation and attitude when I go to church?

PRAYER

Lord, help me to avail of the penitential sacraments during this season of Lent as a means of cleansing myself and coming closer to you.

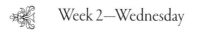

Being Honest with Jesus

But Jesus on his part would not entrust himself to
them, because he knew all people and needed no one
to testify about anyone; for he himself knew what
was in everyone.

—John 2:24–25

Can Jesus trust himself to me? Can Jesus trust me, or
am I two-faced? Do I play the Catholic, one close
to the Church, and then live as a pagan? "But Jesus
doesn't know, no one goes and tells him about it." . . .
Jesus knows all that there is in our heart. We cannot
deceive Jesus. In front of him, we cannot pretend to be
saints . . . and then live a life that is not what he wants.

It will do us good to enter our hearts and look at
Jesus. To say to him: "Lord, look, there are good things,
but there are also things that aren't good. Jesus, do you

trust me? I am a sinner." . . . This doesn't scare Jesus. If you tell him: "I'm a sinner," it doesn't scare him. What distances him is one who is two-faced: showing him or herself as just in order to cover up hidden sin. . . . If your heart isn't just, if you don't do justice, if you don't love those who need love, if you do not live according to the spirit of the Beatitudes, you are not Catholic. You are a hypocrite. First: can Jesus trust himself to me? In prayer, let us ask him: Lord, do you trust me?

Homily, March 8, 2015

REFLECTION

When I look at my life, do I see a disconnect between what I think, say, and do?

PRAYER

Help me to be honest with you, Lord, trusting that you love me as I am.

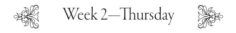
God's Mercy Cleanses

Making a whip of cords, he [Jesus] drove all of them out of the temple, both the sheep and the cattle. He also poured out the coins of the money changers and overturned their tables.

—John 2:15

When we enter our hearts, we find things that aren't okay, things that aren't good, as Jesus found that filth of profiteering, of the profiteers, in the temple. Inside of us too, there are unclean things, there are sins of selfishness, of arrogance, pride, greed, envy, jealousy . . . so many sins! . . . "Jesus . . . I open the door to you; you cleanse my soul." Ask the Lord that as he went to cleanse the temple, he may come to cleanse your soul. We imagine that he comes with a whip of cords. . . . No, he doesn't cleanse the soul with that! Do you know what kind of whip Jesus uses to cleanse our soul? Mercy. Open your heart to Jesus' mercy! Say: "Jesus, look how much filth! Come, cleanse. Cleanse with your mercy, with your tender words, cleanse with your caresses." If we open our heart to Jesus' mercy, in order to cleanse our heart, our soul, Jesus will trust himself to us.

Homily, March 8, 2017

REFLECTION

Dare I open my heart to show Jesus the areas of my life where I need his mercy?

PRAYER

Lord, come into my life with your divine mercy and renew my faith in your merciful love.

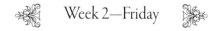

Our Life as a Temple of God

Or do you not know that your body is a temple of the
Holy Spirit within you . . . ?

—1 Corinthians 6:19

Let us walk in the world as Jesus did, and let us make
our whole existence a sign of our love for our brothers, especially the weakest and poorest; *let us build for
God a temple of our lives. . . .* If we are witnesses of the
living Christ, so many people will encounter Jesus in us,
in our witness. But, we ask — . . . does the Lord feel at
home in my life? Do we allow him to "cleanse" our hearts
and to drive out . . . those attitudes of cupidity, jealousy,
worldliness, envy, hatred, those habits of gossiping and
tearing down others? Do I allow him to cleanse all the
behaviors that are against God, against our neighbor,
and against ourselves . . . ?

Every Eucharist that we celebrate with faith makes us grow as a living temple of the Lord, thanks to the communion with his crucified and risen Body. Jesus recognizes what is in each of us, and knows well our most ardent desires: that of being inhabited by him, only by him. Let us allow him to enter into our lives, into our families, into our hearts.

Angelus, March 8, 2015

REFLECTION

When people meet me, do they see a living temple of God?

PRAYER

Lord, may your grace and love transform me so that it's no longer I that live, but you who live in me (see Gal 2: 20).

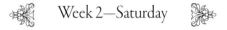

Week 2—Saturday

God's Infinite Patience

He said to the gardener, "For three years I have come looking for fruit on this fig tree, and still I find none. Cut it down!" . . . He replied, "Sir, let it alone for one more year, until I dig around it . . . If it bears fruit next year, well and good."

—Luke 13:8–9

Jesus . . . invites us to change our heart, to make a radical about-face on the path of our lives, to abandon compromises with evil . . . in order to decidedly take up the path of the Gospel. But . . . there is the temptation to justify ourselves. What should we convert from? Aren't we basically good people? How many times have we thought this: "But after all I am a good man, I'm a good woman" . . . Am I not a believer and even quite a churchgoer?" . . .

Unfortunately, each of us strongly resembles the tree that, over many years, has repeatedly shown that it's infertile. But, fortunately for us, Jesus is like a farmer who, with limitless patience, still obtains a concession for the fruitless vine. . . .

It's never too late to convert, never. . . . God's patience awaits us until the last moment. . . . He saves us because he has great patience with us.

Angelus, February 28, 2016

REFLECTION

What is stopping me from repenting of my sins?

PRAYER

Lord, help me not to take your patience for granted. Give me a sense of urgency to repent and start anew.

WEEK 3

Walking in the Light

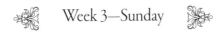
Jesus Quenches Our Thirst

"Sir, give me this water, so that I may never be thirsty
or have to keep coming here to draw water."

—John 4:15

The water that gives eternal life was poured into our
hearts on the day of our Baptism; then God transformed and filled us with his grace. But we may have
forgotten this great gift that we received . . . and perhaps
we seek "wells" whose water does not quench our thirst.
When we forget the true water, we go in search of wells
that do not have clean water. . . .

Jesus speaks to us as he does to the Samaritan
woman. Of course, we already know him, but perhaps
we have not yet encountered him personally . . . [and]
have not recognized him as our Savior. Lent is a good

occasion to draw near to him, to encounter him in prayer in a heart-to-heart dialogue . . . It is a good occasion to see his face in the face of a suffering brother or sister. In this way we can renew in ourselves the grace of Baptism, quench our thirst at the wellspring of the Word of God and of his Holy Spirit; and in this way, also discover the joy of becoming artisans of reconciliation and instruments of peace in daily life.

Angelus, March 19, 2017

REFLECTION

What am I thirsting for and where are the wells where I quench my thirst?

PRAYER

Lord, let me drink your living water so that I may know you as my Savior and become more like you each day.

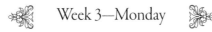

Be Merciful Like the Father

But while he was still far off, his father saw him and was filled with compassion; he ran and put his arms around him and kissed him.

—Luke 15:20

The figure of the Father in the parable reveals the heart of God. He is the merciful Father who, in Jesus, loves us beyond measure, always awaits our conversion every time we make mistakes; he awaits our return when we turn away from him thinking we can do without him; he is always ready to open his arms no matter what happened. As the father of the Gospel, God also continues to consider us his children, even when we get lost, and comes to us with tenderness when we return to him. . . . The errors we commit . . . do not wear out the fidelity of his love. In the Sacrament of Reconciliation, we can always start out anew. He welcomes us, gives us the dignity of being his children and tells us: "Go ahead! Be at peace! Rise, go ahead!"

Angelus, March 6, 2016

REFLECTION

How can I love others the way God loves me?

PRAYER

Lord Jesus, when I am unable to forgive or be merciful to others, gently remind me of God's mercy to me.

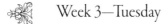

Walking in the Light

[Jesus said to him,] "Go, wash in the pool of Siloam" (which means Sent). Then he went and washed and came back able to see.

—John 9:7

Baptism . . . is the first sacrament of faith: the sacrament which makes us "come to the light," by being reborn through the water and through the Holy Spirit. . . .

The man born blind and healed represents us when we do not realize that Jesus is the light, he is "the Light of the World," when we are looking elsewhere, when we prefer to entrust ourselves to little lights, when we are groping in the dark. . . . We too have been *illuminated* by Christ in Baptism, and thus we are called to behave as children of the light. Acting as children of the light requires a radical change of mind-set, a capacity to judge men and things according to another scale of values, which comes from God. The Sacrament of Baptism, in fact, requires the choice of living as children of the light and walking in the light.

Angelus, March 26, 2017

REFLECTION

Do I judge the things of the world and the people I encounter according to the values of the world or in the light of Christ?

PRAYER

Lord, let your light illuminate the dark areas of my life and show me where I need to change.

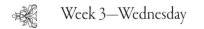

We Are Children of Light

"I am the light of the world."

—John 9:5

Jesus manifests himself . . . to us as the Light of the World. What does it mean to have the true light, to *walk in the light?* First of all it means abandoning false lights: the cold, vain light of prejudice against others, because prejudice distorts reality and ladens us with aversion to those whom we judge without mercy and condemn without appeal. . . . When you gossip about others, you do not walk in the light, you walk in shadows. Another false light, because it is seductive and ambiguous, is that of self-interest: if we value men and things on the basis of usefulness to us, of pleasure, of prestige, we are not truthful in our relationships and situations. If we go down this path of seeking self-interest, we are walking in shadows.

May the Blessed Virgin, who was the first to welcome Jesus, the Light of the World, obtain for us the grace of welcoming anew the light of faith this Lent . . . May this new illumination transform us in attitude and action, so that we too . . . may be bearers of a ray of the light of Christ.

Angelus, March 26, 2017

REFLECTION

How can I bring the light of Christ to the people around me?

PRAYER

Lord, help me to bear your light with humility and love.

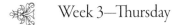

Saved by His Grace

The scribes and the Pharisees brought a woman who had been caught in adultery . . . making her stand before all of them.

—John 8:3

That woman represents all of us. We are sinners, meaning adulterers, before God, betrayers of his fidelity. Her experience represents God's will for each of us: not our condemnation but our salvation through Jesus. He is the grace which saves from sin and from death. On the ground, in the dust of which every human being is made (see Gen 2:7), he wrote God's sentence: "I want not that you die but that you live." God does not nail us to our sin, he does not identify us by the evil we have committed. We have a name, and God does not identify this name with the sin we have committed. He wants to free us, and wants that we too want it together with him. He wants us to be free to convert from evil to good, and this is possible—it is possible!—with his grace.

Angelus, March 13, 2016

REFLECTION

Do I allow God's grace to work in my life to free me from sin and despair?

PRAYER

Lord, you love me as I am. Help me to cooperate with your grace to do good in the world.

Week 3—Friday

Jesus Is Our New Life

"Lazarus, come out!"

– John 11:43

We hear directed to each one of us Jesus' words to Lazarus: "Come out." Come out from the gridlock of hopeless sadness; unwrap the bandages of fear that impede the journey, the laces of the weaknesses and anxieties that constrain you; reaffirm that God unties the knots. By following Jesus, we learn not to knot our lives around problems which become tangled. There will always be problems, always, and when we solve one, another one duly arrives. We can however, find *a new stability*, and this stability is Jesus himself. This stability is called Jesus, who is the Resurrection and the Life. With him, joy abides in our hearts, hope is reborn, suffering is transformed into peace, fear into trust, hardship into an offering of love. And even though burdens will not disappear, there will always be his uplifting hand, his encouraging Word saying to all of us, to each of us: "Come out! Come to me!" He tells all of us: "Do not be afraid."

Homily, April 2, 2017

REFLECTION

What are my fears that drain the joy, hope, and love from my life?

PRAYER

Jesus, Lord of the Resurrection, enliven me to come out of the fearful darkness in my life.

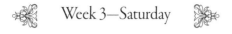

Week 3—Saturday

The Abundance of God's Mercy

Have mercy upon us, O Lord, have mercy upon us.
—Psalm 123:3

The mercy of our God is infinite and indescribable. We express the power of this mystery as an "ever greater" mercy . . . a mercy that each day seeks to make progress, taking small steps forward and advancing in that wasteland where indifference and violence have predominated. . . .

Every one of us, looking at our own lives as God does, can try to remember the ways in which the Lord has been merciful toward us, how he has been much more merciful than we imagined. In this we can find the courage to ask him to take a step further and to reveal yet more of his mercy in the future. . . . This paradoxical way of praying to an ever more merciful God helps us to tear down those walls with which we try to contain the abundant greatness of his heart. It is good for us to break out of our set ways, because it is proper to the heart of God to overflow with tenderness, with ever more to give. For the Lord prefers something to be wasted rather than one drop of mercy be held back. He would rather have many seeds be carried off by the birds of the air than have one seed be missing, since each of those seeds has the capacity to bear abundant fruit, thirtyfold, sixtyfold, even a hundredfold.

Homily, March 24, 2016

REFLECTION

Do I measure out mercy like a miser, or do I share it generously?

PRAYER

Lord, let your all-encompassing love for me inspire me to share this love with others.

WEEK 4

The Good News Leads Us to Joy

The Good News as Contagious Joy

"No one puts new wine into old wineskins; otherwise the new wine will burst the skins and will be spilled, and the skins will be destroyed."

—Luke 5:37

The joys of the Gospel are special joys. . . . They need to be poured into new wineskins, the ones the Lord speaks of in expressing the newness of his message. I would like to share with you . . . three images or icons of those new wineskins* in which the *good news* is kept fresh . . .

A first icon of the good news would be the stone water jars at the wedding feast of Cana (see Jn 2:6). In one way, they clearly reflect that perfect vessel which is Our Lady herself, the Virgin Mary. The Gospel tells us

---

* See the following reflections for the second and third icons.

that the servants "filled them up to the brim" (Jn 2:7)....
Mary is the new wineskin brimming with contagious
joy.... She is "the handmaid of the Father who sings his
praises" (*Evangelii Gaudium,* 286), Our Lady of Prompt
Succor, who, after conceiving in her immaculate womb
the Word of life, goes out to visit and assist her cousin
Elizabeth. Her "contagious fullness" helps us overcome
the temptation of fear, the temptation to keep ourselves
from being filled to the brim and even overflowing, the
temptation to a faint-heartedness that holds us back
from going forth to fill others with joy. This cannot be,
for "the joy of the Gospel fills the hearts and lives of all
who encounter Jesus" (*Evangelii Gaudium,* 1).

Homily, April 13, 2017 (Chrism Mass)

(Part 1 of 3 parts)

REFLECTION

What are some ways I can reach out to others with
the good news of the Gospel?

PRAYER

Lord, infect me with the contagious joy of the Gospel
so that I may proclaim it boldly in word and deed.

The Good News as Inclusive Action

[Jesus said], "The water that I will give will become
in them a spring of water gushing up to eternal life."
The woman said to him, "Sir, give me this water, so
that I may never be thirsty."

—John 4:14–15

A second icon of the *good news** . . . is the jug with its
wooden ladle that the Samaritan woman carried
on her head in the midday sun (see Jn 4:5–30). It speaks
to us of something crucial: the importance of concrete
situations. The Lord, the Source of Living Water, had no
means of drawing the water to quench his thirst. So the
Samaritan woman drew the water with her jug, and with
her ladle she sated the Lord's thirst. She sated it even
more by concretely confessing her sins. By mercifully

---

* See the previous and following reflections for the first and third icons.

shaking the vessel of that Samaritan woman's soul, the Holy Spirit overflowed upon all the people of that small town, who asked the Lord to stay with them.

The Lord gave us another . . . wineskin full of this "inclusive concreteness" in that Samaritan soul who was Mother Teresa. He called to her and told her: "I am thirsty." He said: "My child, come, take me to the hovels of the poor. Come, be my light. I cannot do this alone. They do not know me, and that is why they do not love me. Bring me to them." Mother Teresa, starting with one concrete person, thanks to her smile and her way of touching their wounds, brought the *good news* to all.

Homily, April 13, 2017

(Part 2 of 3 parts)

REFLECTION

What are some concrete acts of service I can do to proclaim the good news?

PRAYER

Lord, give me empathy to know how to reach out with thoughtful actions to those who are excluded in society.

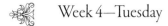

The Good News as Utter Meekness

When they look on the one] whom they have pierced, they shall mourn for him, as one mourns for an only child, and weep bitterly over him.

—Zechariah 12:10

The third icon of the *good news** is the fathomless vessel of the Lord's pierced heart: his utter meekness, humility, and poverty which draw all people to himself. From him we have to learn that announcing a great joy to the poor can only be done in a respectful, humble, and even humbling way. Concrete, tender, and humble: in this way our evangelization will be joyful. Evangelization cannot be presumptuous, nor can the integrity of the truth be rigid, because truth became

---

* See the previous two reflections for the first and second icons.

flesh, it became tenderness, it became a child, it became a man and, on the cross, it became sin (see 2 Cor 5:21). The Spirit proclaims and teaches "the whole truth" (see Jn 16:13), and he is not afraid to do this one sip at a time. The Spirit tells us in every situation what we need to say to our enemies (see Mt 10:19), and at those times he illumines our every small step forward. This meekness and integrity gives joy to the poor, revives sinners, and grants relief to those oppressed by the devil.

Homily, April 13, 2017
(Part 3 of 3 parts)

REFLECTION

Can I take some time to contemplate the pierced side of Jesus on the Cross, and let this move me to a greater love for him and for others?

PRAYER

Fill me with a love for the poor, sweet Jesus.

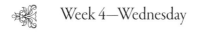

Week 4—Wednesday

Daily Works of Mercy

"Be merciful, just as your Father is merciful."

—Luke 6:36

It is not enough to experience God's mercy in one's life; whoever receives it must also become a sign and instrument for others. Mercy, therefore, is not only reserved for particular moments, but it embraces our entire daily existence.

How can we . . . be witnesses of mercy? . . . The Lord shows us a very simple path, made by small actions which, nonetheless, have great value in his eyes, to the extent to which he has told us that it is by these actions we will be judged. . . . Jesus says that every time we give food to the hungry and drink to the thirsty, clothe the naked and welcome the foreigner, visit the sick or imprisoned, we do the same to him (see Mt 25:31–46). The Church calls these actions *corporal works of mercy,* because they assist people with their material necessities.

There are also . . . *seven other works of mercy called "spiritual,"* which pertain to other equally important needs, especially today, because they touch the person's soul, and often create the greatest suffering. . . . [These are] bear wrongs patiently . . . counsel the doubtful, instruct the ignorant, admonish sinners, console the afflicted, pardon offenses, pray to God for the living and the dead. These are daily things!

General Audience, October 12, 2016

Reflection

Which of these works of mercy am I most drawn to? Can I resolve to show mercy daily through these works?

Prayer

Lord, thank you for the reminder that it is easy to be an instrument of mercy in my day-to-day living.

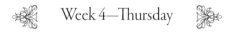 Week 4—Thursday

Steadfast in Our Hope

Strengthen your hearts, for the coming of the Lord is near.

—James 5:8

As individuals too, we are tempted by indifference. Flooded with news reports and troubling images of human suffering, we often feel our complete inability to help. What can we do to avoid being caught up in this spiral of distress and powerlessness?

First, we can pray in communion with the Church on earth and in heaven. . . .

Second, we can help by acts of charity, reaching out to both those near and far through the Church's many charitable organizations. Lent is a favorable time for showing this concern for others by small yet concrete signs of our belonging to the one human family.

Third, the suffering of others is a call to conversion, since their need reminds me of the uncertainty of my own life and my dependence on God and my brothers and sisters. If we humbly implore God's grace and accept our own limitations, we will trust in the infinite possibilities which God's love holds out to us. We will also be able to resist the diabolical temptation of thinking that by our own efforts we can save the world and ourselves.

Message for Lent 2015

REFLECTION

What gives me a sense of hope in the face of human suffering?

PRAYER

Lord, help me focus on the things I can control when I feel hopeless—such as my actions and attitudes—confident that your love will guide me to do the right things.

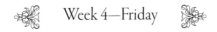
Each Person Is a Gift

"There was a rich man who was dressed in purple and fine linen and who feasted sumptuously every day. And at his gate lay a poor man named Lazarus, covered with sores, who longed to satisfy his hunger with what fell from the rich man's table."

—Luke 16:19–21

Lazarus teaches us that *other persons are a gift*. A right relationship with people consists in gratefully recognizing their value. Even the poor person at the door of the rich is not a nuisance, but a summons to conversion and to change. The parable first invites us to open the doors of our heart to others because each person is a gift, whether it be our neighbor or an anonymous pauper. Lent is a favorable season for opening the doors to all those in need and recognizing in them the face of Christ.

Each of us meets people like this every day. Each life that we encounter is a gift deserving acceptance, respect, and love. The word of God helps us to open our eyes to welcome and love life, especially when it is weak and vulnerable. But in order to do this, we have to take seriously what the Gospel tells us about the rich man.

Message for Lent 2017

REFLECTION

How can I treat people as the unique gifts from God that they truly are?

PRAYER

Thank you Lord for the gift of each one of us and help me to treasure everyone I meet.

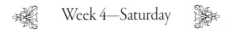
God's Mercy Clothes Our Misery

[Jesus said] "Woman, where are they? Has no one condemned you? . . . Neither do I condemn you. Go your way, and from now on do not sin again."

—John 8:10–11

This Gospel account . . . is not an encounter of sin and judgment in the abstract, but of a sinner and her Savior. Jesus looked that woman in the eye and read in her heart a desire to be understood, forgiven, and set free. The misery of sin was clothed with the mercy of love. Jesus' only judgment is one filled with mercy and compassion for the condition of this sinner. To those who wished to judge and condemn her to death, Jesus replies with a lengthy silence. His purpose was to let God's voice be heard in the consciences not only of the woman, but also in those of her accusers, who drop their

stones and one by one leave the scene (see Jn 8:9). . . .
Jesus helps the woman to look to the future with hope
and to make a new start in life. Henceforth, if she so
desires, she can "walk in charity" (Eph 5:2). Once
clothed in mercy, even if the inclination to sin remains, it
is overcome by the love that makes it possible for her to
look ahead and to live her life differently.

Apostolic Letter Misericordia et Misera *at the Conclusion of
the Extraordinary Jubilee of Mercy, November 20, 2016*

REFLECTION

Do I treat with mercy and compassion those who
live on society's fringes—the criminal, the drunk, the
migrant, the outcast?

PRAYER

Lord, when I feel inclined to judge others by my
own standards, help me to put myself in their situation
and to pray for your loving mercy to clothe and transform us all.

WEEK 5

The Time of Mercy

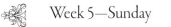

Loved and Forgiven

"Her sins, which were many, have been forgiven; hence she has shown great love. But the one to whom little is forgiven, loves little."

—Luke 7:47

*F*orgiveness is the most visible sign of the Father's love, which Jesus sought to reveal by his entire life. Every page of the Gospel is marked by this imperative of a love that loves to the point of forgiveness. Even at the last moment of his earthly life, as he was being nailed to the cross, Jesus spoke words of forgiveness: "Father, forgive them; for they know not what they do" (Lk 23:34).

Nothing of what a repentant sinner places before God's mercy can be excluded from the embrace of his forgiveness. For this reason, none of us has the right to make forgiveness conditional.

Mercy is always a gratuitous act of our heavenly Father, an unconditional and unmerited act of love. Consequently, we cannot risk opposing the full freedom of the love with which God enters into the life of every person. Mercy is this concrete action of love that, by forgiving, transforms and changes our lives. In this way, the divine mystery of mercy is made manifest. God is merciful (see Ex 34:6); his mercy lasts forever (see Ps 136). From generation to generation, it embraces all those who trust in him and it changes them, by bestowing a share in his very life.

Apostolic Letter Misericordia et Misera *at the Conclusion of the Extraordinary Jubilee of Mercy, November 20, 2016*

REFLECTION

Do I bear any grudges in my heart? If so, how can I surrender them to Jesus?

PRAYER

Lord, may your love for me help me to be generous in forgiving others.

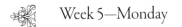

The Time for Mercy Is Upon Us

Once you had not received mercy, but now you have received mercy."

—1 Peter 2:10

This is the time of mercy. Each day of our journey is marked by God's presence. He guides our steps with the power of the grace that the Spirit pours into our hearts to make them capable of loving. *It is the time of mercy* for each and all, since no one can think that he or she is cut off from God's closeness and the power of his tender love. *It is the time of mercy* because those who are weak and vulnerable, distant and alone, ought to feel the presence of brothers and sisters who can help them in their need. *It is the time of mercy* because the poor should feel that they are regarded with respect and concern by others who have overcome indifference and discovered what is essential in life. *It is the time of mercy* because no sinner can ever tire of asking forgiveness and all can feel the welcoming embrace of the Father.

Apostolic Letter Misericordia et Misera *at the Conclusion of the Extraordinary Jubilee of Mercy, November 20, 2016*

REFLECTION

How do I help to bring God's mercy to the people who need it most?

PRAYER

Lord, you are always stretching out your hand of mercy to each one of us. Help me to be your extended hand of mercy to those whom I meet.

Mercy in Forgiveness

"So my heavenly Father will also do to every one of you, if you do not forgive your brother or sister from your heart."

—Matthew 18:35

This parable contains a profound teaching for all of us. Jesus affirms that mercy is not only an action of the Father; it becomes a criterion for ascertaining who his true children are. In short, we are called to show mercy because mercy has first been shown to us. Pardoning offenses becomes the clearest expression of merciful love, and for us Christians it is an imperative from which we cannot excuse ourselves. At times how hard it seems to forgive! And yet pardon is the instrument placed into our fragile hands to attain serenity of heart. To let go of anger, wrath, violence, and revenge are necessary conditions to living joyfully. Let us therefore heed the Apostle's exhortation: "Do not let the sun go down on your anger" (Eph 4:26). Above all, let us listen to the words of Jesus who made mercy an ideal of life and a criterion for the credibility of our faith: "Blessed are the merciful, for they shall obtain mercy" (Mt 5:7).

Bull of Indiction Misericordiae Vultus
of the Extraordinary Jubilee of Mercy, April 11, 2015

REFLECTION

How can forgiveness lead me to a joyful and serene heart?

PRAYER

Jesus, help me witness to my faith through the forgiveness I show others.

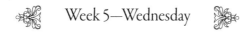
Works of Mercy

"Truly I tell you, just as you did it to one of the least
of these who are members of my family, you did it to
me."

—Matthew 25:40

We cannot escape the Lord's words to us, and they
will serve as the criteria upon which we will be
judged: whether we have fed the hungry and given drink
to the thirsty, welcomed the stranger and clothed the
naked, or spent time with the sick and those in prison
(see Mt 25:31–46). Moreover, we will be asked if we
have helped others to escape the doubt that causes them
to fall into despair and which is often a source of loneli-
ness; if we have helped to overcome the ignorance in
which millions of people live, especially children
deprived of the necessary means to free them from the

bonds of poverty; if we have been close to the lonely and afflicted; if we have forgiven those who have offended us and have rejected all forms of anger and hate that lead to violence; if we have had the kind of patience God shows, who is so patient with us; and if we have commended our brothers and sisters to the Lord in prayer. In each of these "little ones," Christ himself is present. His flesh becomes visible in the flesh of the tortured, the crushed, the scourged, the malnourished, and the exiled . . . to be acknowledged, touched, and cared for by us. Let us not forget the words of Saint John of the Cross: "as we prepare to leave this life, we will be judged on the basis of love" (*Words of Light and Love*, 57).

Bull of Indiction Misericordiae Vultus
of the Extraordinary Jubilee of Mercy, April 11, 2015

REFLECTION

Which saints can I emulate in works of charity?

PRAYER

Lord, help me to see the many different ways I can serve you through ministering to others.

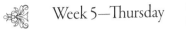
Mercy and Justice

"I desire steadfast love and not sacrifice."

—Hosea 6:6

Mercy is not opposed to justice but rather expresses God's way of reaching out to the sinner, offering him a new chance to look at himself, convert, and believe. . . . If God limited himself to only justice, he would cease to be God, and would instead be like human beings who ask merely that the law be respected. But mere justice is not enough. Experience shows that an appeal to justice alone will result in its destruction. This is why God goes beyond justice with his mercy and forgiveness. Yet this does not mean that justice should be devalued or rendered superfluous. On the contrary: anyone who makes a mistake must pay the price. However, this is just the beginning of conversion, not its end, because one begins to feel the tenderness and mercy of God. God does not deny justice. He rather envelops it and surpasses it. . . . God's justice is his mercy given to everyone as a grace that flows from the death and resurrection of Jesus Christ. Thus the Cross of Christ is God's judgment on all of us and on the whole world, because through it he offers us the certitude of love and new life.

Bull of Indiction Misericordiae Vultus
of the Extraordinary Jubilee of Mercy, April 11, 2015

REFLECTION

How does God's justice assure that mercy will not degenerate into ignoring the pain of those who have suffered from the actions of others?

PRAYER

Lord, help me to know how to balance mercy and justice in my dealings with others.

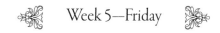

Week 5—Friday

Accepting God's Forgiveness

But when Simon Peter saw it, he fell down at Jesus' knees, saying, "Go away from me, Lord, for I am a sinful man!"

—Luke 5:8

God does not only forgive incalculable debts . . . he also enables us to move directly from the most shameful disgrace to the highest dignity without any intermediary stages. . . . As soon as Simon confesses his sin and begs Jesus to send him away, the Lord raises him to be a fisher of men. We, however, tend to separate these two attitudes: when we are ashamed of our sins, we hide ourselves and walk around with our heads down . . . and when we are raised up to some dignity, we try to cover up our sins and take pleasure in being seen, almost showing off.

Our response to God's superabundant forgiveness should be always to preserve *that healthy tension between a dignified shame and a shamed dignity.* It is the attitude of one who seeks a humble and lowly place, but who can also allow the Lord to raise him up for the good of the mission, without complacency. The model that the Gospel consecrates, and which can help us when we confess our sins, is Peter, who allowed himself to be questioned about his love for the Lord, but who also renewed his acceptance of the ministry of shepherding the flock which the Lord had entrusted to him.

Homily, March 24, 2016

REFLECTION

What is my attitude to my sinfulness and God's forgiveness?

PRAYER

Lord, help me to remember Saint Peter each time I fall into sin: eager to repent and thankful for God's mercy.

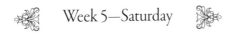

Actions Speak Louder

Little children, let us love, not in word or speech, but in truth and action.

—1 John 3:18

Love, therefore, is the *practical service* that we offer to others. Love is not a word, it is a deed, a service; *humble* service, *hidden* and *silent*, like Jesus said himself: "do not let your left hand know what your right hand is doing" (Mt 6:3). It entails putting at others' disposal the gifts that the Holy Spirit has given us, so that the community might thrive (see 1 Cor 12:4–11). Furthermore, it is expressed in the *sharing* of material goods, so that no one be left in need. This sharing with and dedication to those in need is the lifestyle that God suggests, even to non-Christians, as the authentic path of humanity.

Audience for Jubilee of Mercy, March 12, 2016

REFLECTION

Is it difficult for me to share what I have with the Church and the larger community? Why or why not?

PRAYER

Thank you, Lord, for the material blessings you have given me. Help me to generously share what you give me with others.

WEEK 6

Jesus Loves Us to the End

Week 6—Palm Sunday

Our King the Suffering Servant

"Blessed is the king who comes in the name of the Lord!"

—Luke 19:38

[T]his] celebration can be said to be bittersweet. It is joyful and sorrowful at the same time. We celebrate the Lord's entrance into Jerusalem to the cries of his disciples who acclaim him as king. Yet we also solemnly proclaim the Gospel account of his Passion. In this poignant contrast, our hearts experience in some small measure what Jesus himself must have felt in his own heart that day, as he rejoiced with his friends and wept over Jerusalem. . . .

So as we joyfully acclaim our King, let us also think of the sufferings that he will have to endure in this week. Let us think of the slanders and insults, the snares and betrayals, the abandonment to an unjust judgment, the blows, the lashes and the crown of thorns. . . . And lastly, the way of the cross leading to the crucifixion.

Homily, April 9, 2017

REFLECTION

Have I been unjustly criticized, slandered, or abandoned? How do I react to these moments of rejection?

PRAYER

Jesus Lord, help me to accept my small crosses as a way to closer union with you.

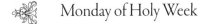

Monday of Holy Week

Putting Others First

We know love by this, that he laid down his life for us—and we ought to lay down our lives for one another.

—1 John 3:16

G od's way of acting may seem so far removed from our own, that he was annihilated for our sake, while it seems difficult for us to even forget ourselves a little. He comes to save us; we are called to choose his way: the way of service, of giving, of forgetfulness of ourselves. Let us walk this path, pausing in these days to gaze upon the crucifix; it is the "royal seat of God." I invite you . . . to gaze often upon this "royal seat of God," to learn about the humble love which saves and gives life, so that we may give up all selfishness, and the seeking of power and fame. By humbling himself, Jesus invites us to walk on his path. Let us turn our faces to him, let us ask for the grace to understand at least something of the mystery of his obliteration for our sake; and then, in silence, let us contemplate the mystery of this Week.

Homily, March 20, 2016

REFLECTION

What are some ways where I put myself before others and how can I change that?

PRAYER

Lord, help me to focus on others more than on myself.

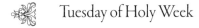 Tuesday of Holy Week

Emptying Myself in Humility

[Christ Jesus] emptied himself, taking the form of a slave, being born in human likeness.

—Philippians 2:7

Humility is above all God's way: God humbles himself to walk with his people, to put up with their infidelity. . . . Following this path to the full, the Son of God took on the *"form of a slave"* (see Phil 2:7). In the end, humility also means *service*. It means making room for God by stripping oneself, "emptying oneself." . . .

In this, we are helped and comforted by the example of so many men and women who, in silence and hiddenness, *sacrifice themselves* daily *to serve others*: a sick relative, an elderly person living alone, a disabled person, the homeless. . . . We think too of the humiliation endured by all those who, for their lives of fidelity to the

Gospel, encounter discrimination and pay a personal price. We think too of our brothers and sisters who are persecuted because they are Christians, *the martyrs of our own time. . . .* They refuse to deny Jesus and they endure insult and injury with dignity. They follow him on his way. Let us set about with determination along this same path of humility, with immense love for him, our Lord and Savior. *Love will guide us and give us strength.*

Homily, March 29, 2015

REFLECTION

What does being humble and accepting humiliation mean to me?

PRAYER

Lord, help my prideful self to follow your example of emptying yourself so that you can fill me with the love of God.

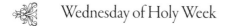

One with Christ in Mercy and Consolation

But God has so arranged the body, giving the greater honor to the inferior member, that there may be no dissension within the body, but the members may have the same care for one another.

—1 Corinthians 12:24–25

Jesus comes to redeem us, to send us out, to transform us from being poor and blind, imprisoned and oppressed, to become ministers of mercy and consolation. He says to us, using the words the prophet Ezekiel spoke to the people who sold themselves and betrayed the Lord: "I will remember my covenant with you in the days of your youth . . . and you shall know that I am the Lord . . . when I forgive you all that you have done, says the Lord God" (Ezek 16:60–63). . . .

We celebrate our Father with hearts full of gratitude, and we pray to him that "he remember his mercy forever"; let us receive, with a dignity that is able to humble itself, the mercy revealed in the wounded flesh of our Lord Jesus Christ. Let us ask him to cleanse us of all sin and free us from every evil. And with the grace of the Holy Spirit let us commit ourselves anew to bringing God's mercy to all men and women, and performing those works which the Spirit inspires in each of us for the common good of the entire people of God.

Homily, March 24, 2016

REFLECTION

How do I comfort the "poor and blind, oppressed and imprisoned" in my life?

PRAYER

Holy Spirit, come into my heart with graces that inspire me to acts of service for others.

Holy Thursday

Cleansed by Jesus' Love

Having loved his own who were in the world, he
loved them to the end.

—John 13:1

Jesus loves us. . . . Jesus' love for us knows no limits. . . .
He never tires of loving anyone. He loves us all, to the
point of giving his life for us. . . . And then, he does something that the disciples don't understand: washing the
feet. In that time . . . it was customary, because when the
people arrived in a home, their feet were dirty with the
dust of the road. . . . And at the entrance to the house,
they washed their feet. It was not done by the master of
the house but by the slaves. . . . And like a slave, Jesus
washes our feet, the feet of his disciples, and that is why
he says: "What I am doing you do not know now, but
afterward you will understand" (Jn 13:7). Jesus' love is so

great that he became a slave to serve us, to heal us, to cleanse us. . . .

When the Lord washes our feet, he washes us entirely, he purifies us, he lets us feel his love yet again. . . . The prophet Isaiah says: "Can a mother forget her child? But even if a mother could forget her child, I will never forget you" (see 49:15). God's love for us is like this.

Homily, April 2, 2015

REFLECTION

How can I grow in love so as to become more self-giving?

PRAYER

Lord, your mercy flows like a river. I want to be cleansed in your mercy and rise to new life.

Good Friday

The Cross on Calvary

Then he handed him over to them to be crucified. So they took Jesus; and carrying the cross by himself, he went out to what is called The Place of the Skull, which in Hebrew is called Golgotha.

—John 19:16–17

Jesus never promised honor and success. The Gospels make this clear. He had always warned his friends that this was to be his path, and that the final victory would be achieved through the passion and the cross. All this holds true for us too. Let us ask for the grace to follow Jesus faithfully, not in words but in deeds. Let us also ask for the patience to carry our own cross, not to refuse it or set it aside, but rather, in looking to him, to take it up and to carry it daily.

Homily, April 9, 2017

REFLECTION

How can I spend this day with Jesus, journeying with him on the road to Calvary?

PRAYER

Lord Jesus, give me the strength to ignore what the world considers success and victory. Help me to be patient with my cross and persevere in carrying it to my Calvary.

 Holy Saturday

Serving Others with Humility

I gave my back to those who struck me, and my cheeks to those who pulled out the beard; I did not hide my face from insult and spitting.

—Isaiah 50:6

May nothing prevent us from finding in [Jesus] the source of our joy, true joy, which abides and brings peace; for it is Jesus alone who saves us from the snares of sin, death, fear and sadness. . . . The Apostle Paul . . . epitomizes in two verbs the path of redemption: Jesus "emptied" and "humbled" himself (Phil 2:7–8). These two verbs show the boundlessness of God's love for us. Jesus *emptied himself:* he did not cling to the glory that was his as the Son of God, but became the Son of man in order to be in solidarity with us sinners in all things; yet he was without sin. Even more, he lived among us in "the condition of a servant" (v. 7); not of a king or a prince, but of a servant. Therefore, he humbled himself, and the abyss of his humiliation . . . seems to be bottomless.

Homily, March 20, 2016

REFLECTION

What acts of service can I do for others today as a sign of my humility and love?

PRAYER

Give me the grace, Lord Jesus, to follow you in humility and service.

EASTER WEEK

The Joy of the Resurrection

The Mystery of Easter

"You are looking for Jesus of Nazareth, who was crucified. He has been raised; he is not here."

—Mark 16:6

We cannot live Easter without entering into the mystery. . . . "To enter into the mystery" means the ability to wonder, to contemplate; the ability to listen to the silence and to hear the tiny whisper amid great silence by which God speaks to us (see 1 Kings 19:12). . . .

To enter into the mystery means going beyond our own comfort zone, beyond the laziness and indifference which hold us back, and going out in search of truth, beauty and love. It is seeking a deeper meaning, an answer, and not an easy one, to the questions which challenge our faith, our fidelity and our very existence.

To enter into the mystery, we need humility, the lowliness to abase ourselves, to come down from the pedestal of our "I" which is so proud, of our presumption; the humility not to take ourselves so seriously, recognizing who we really are: creatures with strengths and weaknesses, sinners in need of forgiveness. To enter into the mystery we need the lowliness that is powerlessness, the renunciation of our idols . . . in a word, we need to adore. Without adoration, we cannot enter into the mystery.

Homily, April 4, 2015

REFLECTION

Can I hear what the Risen Lord is telling me in the silence of his resurrection?

PRAYER

Jesus, Savior of the world, proclaim into my heart the joy of your resurrection.

 Easter Sunday

Transformed by the Resurrection

And suddenly there was a great earthquake . . . the angel said to the women, "Do not be afraid; [Jesus] is not here; for he has been raised, as he said."

—Matthew 28:2–6

L ife, which death destroyed on the cross, now reawakens and pulsates anew (see Romano Guardini, *The Lord*, Chicago, 1954, p. 473). The heartbeat of the Risen Lord is granted us as a gift, a present, a new horizon . . . and we are asked to give it in turn as a transforming force, as the leaven of a new humanity. In the resurrection, Christ rolled back the stone of the tomb, but he wants also to break down all the walls that keep us locked in our sterile pessimism, in our carefully constructed ivory towers that isolate us from life, in our compulsive need for security and in boundless ambition that can make us compromise the dignity of others.

When the High Priest and the religious leaders, in collusion with the Romans, believed that . . . the final word had been spoken and that it was up to them to apply it, God suddenly breaks in . . . and offers new possibilities. God once more comes to meet us, to create and consolidate a new age, the age of mercy. This is the promise present from the beginning. This is God's surprise for his faithful people. Rejoice! Hidden within your life is a seed of resurrection, an offer of life ready to be awakened.

Homily, April 15, 2017

REFLECTION

In what ways can I witness to the new life that Jesus gives me?

PRAYER

Jesus, Risen Lord, come into my life to break down walls that keep me apart from those who are different from me. Help me to see that we share a common humanity.

The New Life of Christ

[Mary Magdalene and the other Mary] left the tomb quickly with fear and great joy, and ran to tell his disciples.

—Matthew 28:8

Christ is alive! That is what quickened the pace of Mary Magdalene and the other Mary. That is what made them return in haste to tell the news (Mt 28:8). That is what made them lay aside their mournful gait and sad looks. They returned to the city to meet with the others.

Now that, like the two women, we have visited the tomb, I ask you to go back with them to the city. Let us all retrace our steps and change the look on our faces. Let us go back with them to tell the news. . . . In all those places where the grave seems to have the final word, where death seems the only way out. Let us go back to proclaim, to share, to reveal that it is true: the Lord is alive! He is living and he wants to rise again in all those faces that have buried hope, buried dreams, buried dignity....

Let us go, then. Let us allow ourselves to be surprised by this new dawn and by the newness that Christ alone can give. May we allow his tenderness and his love to guide our steps. May we allow the beating of his heart to quicken our faintness of heart.

Homily, April 15, 2017

REFLECTION

Where do I need God's help to be a part of his community of Easter people?

PRAYER

Risen Lord, fill me with your wisdom on how to encourage the people I meet with your new Life.

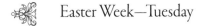

The Risen Christ Lights Up Our Darkness

Mary Magdalene went and announced to the disciples, "I have seen the Lord."

—John 20:18

This . . . is the proclamation that the Church repeats from the first day: *"Christ is risen!"* And in him, through baptism, we too are risen, we have passed from death to life, from the slavery of sin to the freedom of love. Behold the good news that we are called to take to others and to every place, inspired by the Holy Spirit. Faith in the resurrection of Jesus and the hope that he brought us is the most beautiful gift that the Christian can and must give to his brothers. To all and to each, therefore, let us not tire of saying: Christ is risen! . . . Let us repeat it with words, but above all with the witness of our lives. . . .

We proclaim the resurrection of Christ when his light illuminates the dark moments of our life and we can share that with others: when we know how to smile with those who smile and weep with those who weep; when we walk beside those who are sad and in danger of losing hope; when we recount our experience of faith with those who are searching for meaning and for happiness. With our attitude, with our witness, with our life, we say: Jesus is risen! Let us say it with all our soul.

Regina Caeli, April 6, 2015

REFLECTION

How can I shine the risen light of Christ on the lives of the weak and marginalized in my community?

PRAYER

Jesus, Light of the World, enkindle the flames of our heart to never tire of proclaiming your love to all we encounter.

Breaking Open Our Tombs of Despair

Early on the first day of the week, while it was still dark, Mary Magdalene came to the tomb and saw that the stone had been removed from the tomb.

—John 20:1

We . . . cannot discover life by being sad, bereft of hope. Let us not stay imprisoned within ourselves, but let us break open our sealed tombs to the Lord . . . so that he may enter and grant us life. Let us give him the stones of our rancor and the boulders of our past, those heavy burdens of our weaknesses and falls. Christ wants to come and take us by the hand to bring us out of our anguish [and] the lack of hope which imprisons us within ourselves. May the Lord free us from this trap, from being Christians without hope, who live as if the Lord were not risen, as if our problems were the center of our lives.

We see and will continue to see problems both within and without. They will always be there. But . . . it is important to shed the light of the Risen Lord upon our problems, and in a certain sense, to "evangelize" them. . . . Let us not allow darkness and fear to distract us and control us; we must cry out to them: the Lord "is not here, but has risen!" (Mt 28:6). He is our greatest joy; he is always at our side and will never let us down.

Homily, March 26, 2016

REFLECTION

What things have I buried in my tomb that make me hopeless and helpless? Can I surrender them to the Risen Lord?

PRAYER

Lord, you have conquered death and sin. Lead me out of the tomb into your risen light.

Harbingers of Hope in the Risen Lord

Hope does not disappoint us, because God's love has been poured into our hearts through the Holy Spirit that has been given to us.

—Romans 5:5

O ur hope ... is not mere optimism, nor a psychological attitude or desire to be courageous. Christian hope is a gift that God gives us if we come out of ourselves and open our hearts to him. This hope does not disappoint us because the Holy Spirit has been poured into our hearts (see Rom 5:5). The Paraclete does not make everything look appealing. He does not remove evil with a magic wand. But he pours into us the vitality of life, which is not the absence of problems, but the certainty of being loved and always forgiven by Christ, who for us has conquered sin, conquered death, and conquered fear.

The Lord is alive and wants to be sought among the living. After having found him, each person is sent out by him to announce the Easter message, to *awaken and resurrect hope* in hearts burdened by sadness, in those who struggle to find meaning in life. [This] is so necessary today. However, we must not proclaim ourselves. Rather, as *joyful servants of hope,* we must announce the Risen One by our lives and by our love; otherwise we will be only an international organization full of followers and good rules, yet incapable of offering the hope for which the world longs.

Homily, March 26, 2016

REFLECTION

How do I bring Easter joy and hope to the people who need to hear the good news?

PRAYER

Lord, your hope does not mean the end of all problems. Give me an assurance of your deep and abiding love no matter what happens.

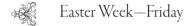

Easter Week—Friday

New Beginnings

So if anyone is in Christ, there is a new creation: everything old has passed away; see, everything has become new!

—2 Corinthians 5:17

We stand before Jesus' empty tomb, and we meditate with wonder and gratitude on the Resurrection of the Lord. Life has conquered death. Mercy and Love have conquered sin! We need faith and hope in order to open ourselves to this new and marvelous horizon. And we know that faith and hope are gifts from God, and we need to ask for them: "Lord, grant me faith, grant me hope! I need them so much!" Let us be permeated by the emotions that resound in the Easter sequence: "Yes, we are sure of it: Christ indeed from death is risen." The Lord has risen among us! . . .

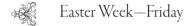

"Christ my hope is arisen!" Since Christ is resurrected, we can look with new eyes and a new heart at every event of our lives, even the most negative ones. Moments of darkness, of failure and even of sin can be transformed and announce the beginning of a new path. When we have reached the lowest point of our misery and our weakness, the Risen Christ gives us the strength to rise again. If we entrust ourselves to him, his grace saves us! The Lord, crucified and risen, is the full revelation of mercy, present and working throughout history.

Regina Caeli, March 28, 2016

REFLECTION

How do I allow the Risen Christ to transform my darkest moments into new beginnings?

PRAYER

Lord, you rose to give us new life. Help me to trust that no matter how many times I may fall, I can always start over with you.

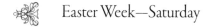 Easter Week—Saturday

Witnessing to Easter Joy

"Then go quickly and tell his disciples, 'He has been raised from the dead.'"

—Matthew 28:7

We feel as if this invitation is also directed to us; to "hasten" and to "go" announce to the men and women of our times this message of joy and hope . . . because from the dawn of the third day, Jesus who was crucified, is raised. Death no longer has the last word. Life does! This is our certainty. . . . This is why we repeat "Christ is Risen" many times. Because in him, the sepulcher was overcome. Life was born.

In light of this event . . . we are called to be new men and women in accordance with the Spirit, *confirming the value of life.* There is life! This is already the beginning of rebirth! We will be men and women of resurrection, men and women of life, if in the midst of the events that afflict the world . . . in the midst of worldliness, which distances us from God, we will know how to offer gestures of solidarity and gestures of welcome, strengthening the universal desire for peace and the hope for an environment free from degradation. These are common and human signs, which if supported and kept alive by faith in the Risen Lord, acquire a power that is well beyond our abilities.

Regina Caeli, April 17, 2017

Reflection

How can I "hasten and go" tell everyone about what the Risen Lord has done in my life?

Prayer

Jesus, Risen Lord, you call me to be your bold witness in the world. Give me the deep desire to accomplish this mission in union with you.

BOOKS & MEDIA

A mission of the Daughters of St. Paul

As apostles of Jesus Christ, evangelizing today's world:

We are CALLED to holiness
by God's living Word and Eucharist.

We COMMUNICATE the Gospel message
through our lives and through all
available forms of media.

We SERVE the Church
by responding to the hopes and needs
of all people with the Word of God,
in the spirit of St. Paul.

For more information visit our website:
www.pauline.org.

Pauline
BOOKS & MEDIA

The Daughters of St. Paul operate book and media centers at the following addresses. Visit, call, or write the one nearest you today, or find us at www.paulinestore.org.

CALIFORNIA
3908 Sepulveda Blvd, Culver City, CA 90230   310-397-8676
3250 Middlefield Road, Menlo Park, CA 94025   650-562-7060

FLORIDA
145 S.W. 107th Avenue, Miami, FL 33174   305-559-6715

HAWAII
1143 Bishop Street, Honolulu, HI 96813   808-521-2731

ILLINOIS
172 North Michigan Avenue, Chicago, IL 60601   312-346-4228

LOUISIANA
4403 Veterans Memorial Blvd, Metairie, LA 70006   504-887-7631

MASSACHUSETTS
885 Providence Hwy, Dedham, MA 02026   781-326-5385

MISSOURI
9804 Watson Road, St. Louis, MO 63126   314-965-3512

NEW YORK
115 E. 29th Street, New York City, NY 10016   212-754-1110

SOUTH CAROLINA
243 King Street, Charleston, SC 29401   843-577-0175

TEXAS
No book center; for parish exhibits or outreach evangelization, contact: 210-569-0500, or SanAntonio@paulinemedia.com, or P.O. Box 761416, San Antonio, TX 78245

VIRGINIA
1025 King Street, Alexandria, VA 22314   703-549-3806

CANADA
3022 Dufferin Street, Toronto, ON M6B 3T5   416-781-9131